SIDE HUSTLE

Retire Early With Multiple Streams Of Passive Income – Make Money With Dropshipping, Amazon Fba, Shopify, Affiliate Marketing, Laundromat, Youtube, Airbnb, Blogging, Etc.

BY CHRISTOPHER KENT

Table of contents

INTRODUCTION

Congratulations on purchasing the book - Side Hustle: Retire Early with Multiple Streams of Passive Income – Make Money with Dropshipping, Airbnb, Shopify, YouTube, Laundromat, Airbnb, Blogging, Amazon FBA, Affiliate Marketing etc.

If you have purchased this book is it because you are ready to start claiming your financial freedom. Maybe you have read about other people doing it, or maybe you have a friend who has done it and as a result, they have an easier time paying the bills while even having some cash leftover at the end of the month. That means that not only are they able to pay their bills with greater ease but they are also able to start paying off debt faster or saving a nest egg for themselves and their family so that they no longer have to worry about finances.

In fact, many people find that they save enough that they can even start to invest it, allowing them to work less and save more. For most people, this is the ultimate goal: no longer having to work while still having passive income coming in from the various streams that they have developed over the years. Then, because of their wise money choices, they are able to start enjoying life more either by doing work that they love or by retiring altogether and spending more time with family enjoying life and traveling.

Either way, no matter what you are looking for or why adding an extra income to your life is always a great idea. In *Side Hustle,* you are going to discover nineteen different side hustles that you can add to your life so that you can start enjoying financial freedom, too. Whether you are looking for something that you can get fully engaged in or something that you can let run without you so that the income is entirely passive, you are bound to find some great ideas in this book.

Side Hustle was written to not only help you identify possible side hustles but also qualify the ones that will suit your needs and ultimately get started with the one that is going to be your next big earner. So, regardless of what you need, if you are looking for an extra $1,000+ per month, you are definitely going to discover exactly how to start.

Are you ready to dive in and find your next side hustle? If so, let's begin!

CHAPTER 1

WHY YOU NEED A SIDE HUSTLE

First things first, let's dig into why you even need a side hustle in the first place. The truth is, there are many reasons why someone would want to have a side hustle in their lives. Side hustles provide extra income that can be used for virtually anything, from travelling more to saving more money to be used toward future expenses like retirement or anything else that you feel you need to get more money going toward. Many people will use side hustles to fund multiple things at once, from debt repayment to enjoying life more on a day to day basis. Truly, there is no right or wrong way to use your side hustle money since it is all just additional money on top of what you already have available to you on a monthly basis.

Most people who have a side hustle also find that they feel more empowered because they have more than just one or two income streams coming into their household. This means that if they needed to take a day off work or even quit their job and find a new one, they would have plenty of money to help them get through that period of time. Knowing that you are not at the mercy of your boss, even if your boss is nice, can feel liberating because it begins to feel like you can make choices for yourself and that no one else can control what you choose to do with your life.

Another big reason why having a side hustle is ideal is because if you use your side hustle correctly you can actually turn that side hustle into a full-time income, even if you are building it passively. This means that if you stay committed and you keep working at it long enough you will begin to discover that your side hustle helps you completely quit your work and enjoy life solely based off of the income you are earning from that side hustle. For many people, this is the goal so they both scale the side hustle and use that income to fund and scale even more side hustles so that, in no time at all, they have plenty of money coming in from various sources funding their lifestyle. This multiple streams of income even from side hustles can be empowering because it means that if ever one does not serve as well one month you can rely on one of your others to help you pull through.

Lastly, side hustles are often started just for money but many people also tie their side hustle into something they love. What can end up happening is you start something because you need extra money but then you discover that you love what you are doing so you keep doing it. As a result, you find yourself not only making money but having a ton of fun doing it which is a huge win for most people. If you are someone who hates your day job, switching into a high paying side gig that you love can be liberating and exhilarating.

If you know that a side hustle is right for you and you are ready to start one, the next nineteen chapters are going to introduce you to excellent side hustles that you can get started with that will help you earn some extra income. Dive in, now!

CHAPTER 2

LAUNDROMAT

Although this may sound oddly specific, laundromats are actually a lucrative business opportunity that can earn you a massive income. Just think about it: all day long people are coming into a laundromat to do laundry and keep their clothes clean. Laundry machines are always needed and, if you are in an area where people tend to use laundromats often, then you can feel confident that your business will stay busy. Read on to learn more about why laundromats are such a great passive income opportunity.

Why Laundromats Work

Coin-operated laundry first started when buildings stopped putting laundry machines into their units and people had to go elsewhere to do laundry. They worked as excellent alternatives because not only did laundromats give people a place to do laundry in the first place, but they also gave people a place to do laundry quickly because people no longer had to wait for one load to be done before starting the next load. Instead, they could run several loads at once and be done their laundry far sooner.

3

Another reason why laundromats are such a great idea is that they do not require you to restock a store or restaurant on a regular basis, meaning that your outgoing expenses are predictable and lower than most other brick and mortar style businesses. This means that you are far more likely to earn profit with coin-operated laundry machines than you are other businesses because all of your clients are putting money right into your pocket and you are putting very little out for it.

Laundromats can be completely passive, too, if you choose to set one up and get someone else working for you. This way, your business can keep running as a complete side hustle while you go ahead and continue working at your job, allowing your laundromat to earn a passive monthly income for you.

What You Need To Get Started

What you will need to start up a laundromat business will ultimately depend on whether you want to be fully engaged with the business or have other people run it entirely. If you want other people to run it entirely it will cost you more because you will have to pay other peoples' wages, however, it also means that you can go about life as usual while your company earns you money. The average cost to start up a laundromat is about $200,000 - $500,000, which will help you acquire a building to run your business in, the machines, and all other business-related tools such as a desk for your attendant and anything else that is needed. You are also going to need to have individuals willing to work for you so that you are not attempting to run the business all on your own as this would no longer be a side hustle. As well, most laundromats are open 6 AM – 10 PM 7 days a week, which means that no one person could reasonably keep up with all of those working hours.

How To Get Started

Starting your laundromat will require you to first identify where a laundromat would be most likely to succeed so that you can purchase or lease a building that is going to be in an ideal area. Remember, people are bringing their laundry to you so they are not going to want to drive terribly far to get to your facilities. Ideally, being around residential buildings that are known for not having laundry machines built-in, such as around a lot of smaller apartments, is a great opportunity for you to put in a laundromat.

In addition to having the right place, you will also need to have the right equipment and staffing to help you get started. You are going to want to purchase as many coin-operated laundry machines as you can fit into your building, as well as other business essentials such as a desk with a chair for your staff, filing systems, and other office supplies to keep your laundromat running. You may also wish to stock small amounts of laundry supplies such as detergents and fabric softener so that people who are not prepared can purchase products from you.

Of course, you are also going to need to go through the process of hiring your staff so you should be prepared to spend at least a few weeks getting your business up and running and training everyone so that you no longer need to be involved. You will likely have to be rather hands-on for the first few months, but once your laundromat is completely running and all of your staff are trained you can go back to being hands-off, allowing the laundromat to become either completely passive or semi-passive.

How Successful You Will Be

Laundromats earn anywhere from $15,000 to $200,000 per year depending on where they are located and how much business they are getting. If you choose the right location for your business you can get people flowing through the door, you can expect to make an average revenue of about $100,00 per year. Fortunately, laundromats do not require many employees, and many do not even have any employees at all but instead simply have one person arrive in the morning to open up and turn on the machines and return at night to shut off the machines. Beyond that, they have a high quality security system that looks after the building. Because of that, operating costs are extremely low meaning that most of that revenue will be kept as profit. The average laundromat owner will keep around $40,000 per year if they make an average of $100,000 per year with their business.

How to Scale Your Business

Naturally, you want to be making closer to $200,000, as opposed to the lower $15,000 that some laundromat owners make per year. For that reason, you want to know exactly how to scale your business. The best way to scale a laundromat business is to ensure that you have the best location possible and that you advertise for your business frequently. As well, adding in extra little amenities like chairs for people to wait in or a vending machine for people to buy drinks or snacks from can make your laundromat more comfortable than others. Beyond that, franchising your business and building more chains is another great opportunity for you to scale your laundromat business so that you can start earning even more.

How Long It Will Take To See Profits

As with most brick and mortar businesses, laundromats will start seeing profits within their second or third year of business. The true amount of time it will take will depend on how successful your location is, how effective your advertising is, and how much you borrowed or invested to get your business up and running.

CHAPTER 3

PUBLISHING BOOKS

Book publishing is an excellent opportunity to earn a passive or semi-passive income. The benefit of book publishing is that, if you want to, you can develop an entire brand around your author name that can eventually be capitalized on, meaning that your side hustle can become a full blown hustle if you want it to. Say, for example, you start selling books that focus on self-help, such as specifically around topics relating to relationships. If you wanted to, then, you could develop a personal brand around relationships that allow you to give relationship advice to people in need. You could then go on to do anything you wanted, from offering products or services meant to help people in relationships. In the end, your book publishing was passive or semi-passive, earned you an income, and opened the door to many new income opportunities that you can now take advantage of.

Why Book Publishing Works

Book publishing works because at the end of the day people love reading. Mostly, people love consuming knowledge about things that are relevant to them or immersing themselves in a fantasy world that takes them away from their own stressors and lets them engage in a different reality for a while. People have been consuming large amounts of books for decades, and although the format for books has switched in a big way, books are still widely popular. Whether people are buying digital books or physical books, virtually everyone owns books and many are still being bought every single day.

Publishing books means that you can get in on that action and start earning a decent income for yourself, too. When you are publishing books, it can take you some time to write them, though the income that you earn after that is passive. As well, if you do not want to write your books yourself, you can always hire a ghostwriter to write them for you. Although this may cost you more up front, having a ghostwriter can make everything a lot more passive in terms of book publishing, meaning that you will earn even more at the end of the day.

What You Need To Get Started

Getting started with writing is inexpensive and typically just takes some time or a small financial investment, depending on what way you want to go. If you want to write the book yourself, you will need $100 for a Microsoft word subscription, $25+ for a book cover, and $50+ for an advertising budget to help you advertise your book when you are ready. This means that you can start for as little as $175. If you want to get someone else to write your book for you it will be a little more costly, with full-service ghostwriters typically starting at $200 and increasing in value from there depending on the length of your book.

How To Get Started

If you want to get started with writing your own book, it is as simple as sitting down with a writing program on your computer and writing out your book. You can write your book in whatever way feels right for you and then go through and edit it later on, or you can hire a writing coach or even purchase a book that guides you through the process. Having a coach or a guide can help you get the layout of your book proper and keep you on track with writing so that you get your entire book written in virtually no time at all. If you want to work with a ghostwriting service, it is as simple as finding the writer you want to work with, letting them know what you are looking for, and paying them for your services.

How Successful You Will Be

How successful you will be will ultimately depend on how well you advertise yourself and how much of a marketing budget you have. The best way to get found as a publisher is to have high quality advertisements and a personal brand developing on social media that helps promote your book so that people have a way of finding you. Unless you are working with a professional publishing agency like Hay House or Harper Collins, you are going to have to be the one getting your book out in front of the masses, which can be costly. You can do this organically through social media and grow over time, or you can invest in a self-publishing service which allows you to receive support from professional marketers and various other tools that help you get your projects out in front of your audience.

How to Scale Your Business

Scaling your publishing business is easy: publish more books. The more that you can publish books and get them out in front of your target audience, the more you are going to have to capitalize on. Keep new books coming out as often as possible, advertise a lot, and build a personal brand so that people can locate you and start following you. Building a loyal following online is a great way to have more people already ready to buy each new book that you publish.

How Long It Will Take To See Profits

You can see profits from your book in as early as 3-6 months depending on how much you invested in the book and how well you are marketing it. After that, everything you earn will be a passive income based on your marketing budget and your growing brand.

CHAPTER 4

DROPSHIPPING

Dropshipping is a great company style where you essentially build an online shop and develop a brand for it and then allow manufacturers to run your business for you. Dropshipping manufacturers are companies who stock products and then ship them directly to your customers from their warehouse. This means that every time someone lands on your website and buys something, your company profits a percentage of that sale for earning the sale for the manufacturer in the first place.

Why Dropshipping Works

Dropshipping works because online shopping is growing massively in popularity and people love shopping online. People love the feeling of ordering something online and receiving it in the mail days later, as it provides a sense of excitement around the shopping experience. As well, since you do not have to store any products or ship anything, you get to save a lot of money which means that the majority of what you earn is profit. In fact, dropshipping businesses are so easy to run that they are essentially a form of passive income, aside from the marketing that you have to do. If you hire a marketing agency to grow your brand for you online, then your dropshipping business will be completely passive.

What You Need To Get Started

To get started with a dropshipping business you are first going to need to find one or two dropshipping companies that you can work with so that you already have products available for you to stock online. Then, you are going to have to get a website developer to design your website for you unless you are already capable of designing your own websites. After that, you are going to need to have a marketing agency who can help you build a brand for and promote your dropshipping company, or at least have a budget for paid advertisements. Ultimately, anything that you are willing to do yourself can save you money, but every element of the dropshipping business can also be outsourced which means that you do not have to do anything. Because of the versatility, starting a dropshipping company can run you anywhere from $500-$10,000+.

How To Get Started

To get started, you first need to determine how much you can or how much you are willing to do on your own. Then, once you know, you can go ahead and start making the necessary connections to get your business going. If you have decided that you want this to be entirely passive and you do not want to do anything then you are going to need to find a dropshipping company to connect with, hire a website developer, hire a marketing agency, and start some basic social media accounts for your brand to be grown on. Once everything is set in place all you have to do is reinvest some of your profits into your marketing agency so that they can continue growing your brand for you. Otherwise, you just sit back and collect your profits at the end of each month.

How Successful You Will Be

Dropshipping can be incredibly successful, or a total flop depending on how well you market your business. The most successful dropshipping companies have great brands online and also have attractive and high quality shopping websites that feel similar to the websites of any other high quality store. Poor quality one-page designs with all of the products lopped onto one page often look like a scam to people so they generally do not do very well. So, if you design your page effectively and your market well, you could be profiting $500-$1000+ per month from a well-designed dropshipping company.

How to Scale Your Business

You can scale a dropshipping business in two different ways: by stocking your store with more products, or by copying your business model and starting additional dropshipping companies that cater to different product niches. If you choose to add more products to your business it will be less expensive, though if you have a successful dropshipping company already and you replicate it, it may be more profitable. You have to decide what way you want to go and how much increased profits you want to see for yourself.

How Long It Will Take To See Profits

With a dropshipping company, it can take about 6-12 months to see your profits. Although you will likely be making money within the first two months, it can take some additional time to break even on side hustles with higher startup investments. If you are not seeing profits in 12 months, you may need to redesign your business or consider switching to something you would be more effective at.

CHAPTER 5

AMAZON FBA

Amazon FBA is similar to dropshipping, except that you will need to be more involved with this business model. If you want to start with Amazon FBA, you are going to need to find the products you want to sell, purchase them from merchants, and have them shipped to Amazon's warehouses. Aside from that, however, nearly everything runs similarly to dropshipping business.

Why Amazon FBA Works

Amazon FBA is a powerful business tool because it allows you to tap into Amazon's built-in marketing program and get everything that you need to sell your products. On Amazon, you have a built-in store, built-in marketing software, and hundreds of thousands of existing customers who are already turning to Amazon to browse the platform to find products just like yours. Plus, you can make Amazon extremely passive by simply having to check in every two to four weeks to ensure that you have enough stock available for your customers. Otherwise, as long as you have a decent marketing budget

16

behind you, you can promote your products easily and remain entirely hands-off.

What You Need To Get Started

Getting started with Amazon FBA is extremely simple. All you need to do is open up an Amazon FBA account, find a manufacturer that you can buy your products from, and get your products shipped to Amazon. Aside from that, you can set up ongoing advertisements with Amazon's marketing software so that your products just keep getting boosted up in people's feeds. They also get seen elsewhere online such as on blogs and on social media, which means that your products will get seen by a massive audience. With these tools in place, you are ready to get started. Getting started with Amazon FBA can be done with as little as $750.

How To Get Started

Once you have a merchant account and an Amazon FBA account with Amazon, all you need to do is have products shipped to Amazon's FBA warehouses. That's it.

How Successful You Will Be

Your Amazon FBA business can be incredibly successful as long as you are willing to invest a fair amount into your initial marketing budget. After you have invested your startup marketing expenses of a couple of hundred dollars, you can expect to sell plenty of products and earn your marketing expenses back and then some in no time at all. Once you have everything up and running you can make anywhere from $1,000 to $10,000+ per month from your Amazon FBA business.

How to Scale Your Business

Scaling your Amazon FBA business is really easy: you simply find more products that you can add to your shop and then you go ahead and you start stocking them. As long as you can afford the manufacturer's fee and you can get them to your Amazon FBA warehouse, your business can expand. The key to massive expansion is to start looking for products that are low cost to acquire and that have a strong profit margin. For example, jewelry can be bought for as little as $1.00 a piece and can be sold for upward of $10 a piece. This is a massive profit margin where you are earning 10x your investment on every piece. Focusing on these types of products will help you scale fast, meaning that you will earn closer to the $10,000+ per month range as long as you scale effectively and in niches where the products are actually desirable.

How Long It Will Take To See Profits

With Amazon FBA, how long it will take for you to see your profits depends on how much stock you buy in the first place. If you buy a lot of stock early on and invest a fair bit into your marketing it could take you a bit longer to see your profits back simply because of how much you have invested. That being said, most people find that they break even and begin to see profits in as little as 3-5 months, assuming that they have entered the business with a strong marketing plan and products that were high in demand.

CHAPTER 6

SHOPIFY BUSINESSES

Shopify businesses are another form of online business that you can run that can help you earn a fair amount of money online. If you run a Shopify business, you can build your own personal brand and have the products in your store branded for you or your company as well. This is a fun way to build an online business with an existing backend platform that allows you to stand out. If you want to make a splash in the world of online retail, Shopify can be a great place to start.

Why Shopify Businesses Work

Shopify gives you the unique advantage of not being up against thousands of other merchants as you would be on a platform like Amazon. Although Shopify has many different businesses running through it, it is also running each business independently with its own store front and web address. This means that people go to a unique domain name to find your store which is not linked to a bigger merchant, like Amazon. The one drawback with a store like this is that you do have to do a lot more marketing for yourself as you do not have existing traffic already eligible to find your products. Instead, you have to make traffic to your domain name for yourself, which can take some time and practice.

What You Need To Get Started

Getting started with Shopify is as easy as opening up an account, sourcing products to sell, purchasing those products, and then launching your business. If you do not want to sell physical products you can always sell digital products which can actually earn you a higher profit because they are cheaper to make and they do not require you to ship anything to your client. Once you have your shop and products available, you are also going to need to go ahead and open up some social media accounts and start branding your business. If you have never branded a business before there are plenty of great guides online, or you might consider getting started with a branding coach or a marketing company who can help you. All that to be considered, starting a Shopify store can cost you anywhere from $750 - $4,000.

How To Get Started

Getting started with your Shopify store is easy. First, you need to decide what brand you want to develop and what niche of products you want to be selling. Since this is all housed under one brand and one store, you want to make sure that all of your products fit into the same niche. Once you have discovered your ideal niche, you need to name your store and start developing a brand for it on social media. You also want to start looking for merchants who sell products that are relevant to your brand so that you can start acquiring products to sell. Ideally, you should have at least 5-10 products in your store to get started so that you are not attempting to market a store with 1-2 items to people. The more products you have to get started with, the better. If you can, consider buying 5-10 of each unique item and then buying a wider range of items so that you can have more variety in your store. This will also allow you to get a better idea of what people are buying from you so that you can stock more of what your audience wants and less of what they do not want.

How Successful You Will Be

Shopify businesses can be wildly successful, earning you $500 - $1000+ per month, with many people regularly making over $5,000 - $10,000 per month with their shop. The big key with Shopify is that you want to make sure that you are effectively marketing your shop so that people can actually find it. If you are not regularly sharing your shop with people and introducing them to what you have available then you are not getting the opportunity to even show them your shop. Having a strong brand online makes all of the difference, as your social media platforms and paid advertisements are how you are going to funnel people to your website. The more people that land there, the better. Because of the necessity of the brand, Shopify can be an income stream that needs quite a bit of your work and involvement to work. However, you can also consider hiring a marketing agency to look after everything so that it is all done for you and you do not have to do anything to get your products in front of other people.

How to Scale Your Business

Scaling your Shopify business comes from scaling your brand and adding more products. As with other online retail shops, the more products that you can stock with larger profit margins, the more you are going to earn. A big way that many Shopify store owners scale their business is by expanding their niche, or by offering highly trending products that people are actively looking for. If you can get your hands on trending products and price them slightly under the average market value, not only will you have something that everyone wants but you will also have one of the best prices. This is a great way to get a massive amount of eyes turned onto your business, fast.

How Long It Will Take To See Profits

With Shopify, it can take closer to 6 months or even a year before you see profits as there is quite a bit that goes into getting a Shopify store profitable. Understand that your profit is heavily reliant on people actually being able to find your store in the first place, as well as them being able to have confidence in the products that you are offering and your brand in general. Most successful brands that are earning large amounts of money have done a lot to earn people's trust, which has resulted in people feeling confident buying from them. Unless you already have a brand, you need to expect to spend some time establishing that trust so that people feel confident buying from you, too. Once you have developed that trust, your profits should start showing up and growing rapidly.

CHAPTER 7

TUTORING

Tutoring is a surprisingly great way to make extra money on the side, although it will take some of your time. Depending on how you do it, tutoring could require all hands on deck, or it could be a semi-passive income stream that you develop to earn money from. If you become a tutor yourself, you are going to be working all the time to earn your money. If, however, you choose to hire other tutors and you simply focus on bringing in clients for those tutors, it can be passive as all you need to do is screen your tutors and market to acquire clients. For this chapter, we are going to talk about what you can do if you are the tutor, and how you can grow your tutoring business.

Why Tutoring Works

Many people want to hire support for themselves or their children to learn about their studies with greater confidence. Learning in classes can be challenging, and sometimes ineffective because there simply is not enough time and attention for lessons to be absorbed and for personal questions to be asked. For that reason, a tutor is a great opportunity for people to get access to that 1:1 help that they may need to help them consume all of the necessary information and feel confident in knowing it. Tutors are always being hired and regularly make $10-$25 per hour in the United States, depending on what you are tutoring on. For example, a tutor for a 5th grade math student will likely earn less than a tutor for a college medical student. Still, many people regularly need help with their studies and you may be able to offer that help by being their tutor.

What You Need To Get Started

Getting started as a tutor is simple and extremely inexpensive. Generally, you can start by having a strong educational background and a few strong connections in your community. You may not even need to do any marketing if you already know of enough people who would benefit from your services, or who could connect you to people who could. For that reason, all you need is a strong network and a solid educational background to get started. You can often start working as a tutor for as little as $0. Even though it is 2019, many people still market their tutoring services on a simple flier smartly placed somewhere locally.

How To Get Started

Getting started as a tutor is simple: connect with someone in your network and get started working with a student! Chances are you are going to need to go through an interview process so that whoever you will be working for knows that you are qualified to educate them on what you are teaching. Your interview will generally be an opportunity for you to introduce yourself, your skills, and your prices so that people know what they can expect from you and if you are the right fit. If you do not know how to price yourself, you can look at other tutors in your area and price yourself accordingly. Alternatively, you might consider looking at a local tutoring agency and get hired through them. For this, you will likely require proof that you are as educated as you say you are, that you are capable of teaching this knowledge, and a criminal record check to ensure that the agency feels confident sending you into their clients' homes. If you work this way, your wage will likely be determined for you by the agency.

How Successful You Will Be

Tutors make an average of $17.50 per hour in the United States, which means that you could be earning around $700 - $1,500 or more per month depending on how much time you are willing to invest in this side hustle. Obviously, the more time you invest the more you are going to earn since tutoring is done on an hourly basis. Most tutors are highly successful, especially if they spend time developing networks in communities of either parents of school aged children or people who are in post-secondary educational programs. The bigger your network, the more likely you are going to be recommended to paying clients so that you can begin working with even more people.

How to Scale Your Business

Scaling your tutoring business can be done either by working more hours or by turning your business into an agency. If you have more clients than you can handle yourself you can always consider turning your business into an agency by hiring other tutors who are qualified to help teach people and earning a percentage of their wages. Then, all you have to do is assign them to your network of people and have them teaching for you. This way, you earn your own wages as well as a percentage of the wages of the tutors that you represent. If you do this, it is important that you set your agency up like an agency and look into your local laws to ensure that you are working within your legal obligations. For example, many agencies like this need to require criminal record checks from their tutors so that they can guarantee that they are not sending criminals into peoples' homes. After all, things like that could come back on you as a liability since you are representing that person through your agency.

How Long It Will Take To See Profits

With tutoring, since it is a $0 start up you can begin seeing profits immediately. Most tutors will require their clients to pay per session, so right from your very first session with a client, you will be earning money. This means that you can start seeing your $1,000+ per month profits in as little as one month as long as you get yourself enough clients working with you.

CHAPTER 8

BLOGGING

Blogging exists in nearly every recommended side hustle list and that is because it works. Many people have argued that blogging is "dead" or that no one reads blogs anymore because they have become so washed out from too many people doing it, but the truth is that blogs are still very much relevant and people are still making $1,000 - $10,000+ per month off of their blogs. If you want to get in on the action, starting your own blog is a great opportunity to have a passion project that earns you big bucks.

Why Blogging Works

Blogging works because people love learning about other people's opinions and reading about other people's lives. Think about it: how many times have you Googled something to discover the answer that you needed? Whether you wanted to know about the latest celebrity buzz or a great recipe that you could cook for under $5, chances are the Google result that you landed on was none other than a blog. Blogs continue to provide high amounts of information for people who are searching for content on the internet. Assuming that you utilize effective SEO measures and talk about something relevant, you can be the one that comes up when people search for a certain subject. As a result, your page grows in popularity which means that money making features like advertisements and sponsored posts begin to earn you a higher income, thus making your blog profitable. Because you are required to write posts for your blog and continue promoting it, blogging is considered to be a semi-passive income stream, although you could make it more passive by hiring writers to write for you if you wanted.

What You Need To Get Started

Getting started with a blog is extremely simple: you can generally start for less than $100 by finding a hosting platform and purchasing a period of hosting time as well as a domain name. Once you have that in place all you have to do is design your blog and begin uploading posts. If you use a platform like Squarespace or Wix, creating your blog is simple as these are click-and-build platforms that allow you to create beautiful websites for inexpensive. Alternatively, if you are more tech savvy or you feel like paying $1,000+ for a website, you can always hire someone to help you create a WordPress website which is typically more customizable but can be significantly more challenging to set up.

How To Get Started

Getting started with your blogging is simple. After you have everything set up, you will want to pick a niche that is relevant to both you and your target audience so that you feel comfortable writing about the topic and people are actually interested in reading about it. If you have never had to pick a niche before, consider looking into something that interests you and then exploring niches related to that subject. You want to choose a niche that has a steady audience that regularly consumes new content to avoid trying to market so hard to a less active audience that will be harder to reach. After you have picked your niche you will want to write 10-15 starter posts for your blog so that you can promote it and give your readers a healthy amount of content to begin reading right away. Then, you want to have a posting schedule so that you are regularly uploading new content on a consistent basis, thus keeping people coming back to your page. Other than that, consistently sharing your content to social media platforms and encouraging people to share the content that they resonate with is the best way to keep your content being seen by your audience.

How Successful You Will Be

A large number of people find great success in blogging for profit, and find that they are earning $200+ per month in the first three months of their blogging career. After that, profits will generally steadily increase until you are earning $1,000+ per month within 6-12 months, depending on how you approach your blog. The big key here is that you need to be uploading and marketing your blog consistently, as this is how you are going to build your reputation and gain credibility. If you do not take the time to consistently get your name out there and show people that you are blogging, chances are you are going to lose credibility fast and therefore your advertisements and sponsored posts will be less valuable. If you want to grow value, you have to build your reputation up and get your audience seeing how trustworthy you are.

How to Scale Your Business

Scaling your blogging business will ultimately come from establishing and developing your blogging reputation, as your blog becomes more valuable the more traffic that you gain on a consistent basis. As you continue to receive increasing amounts of traffic on your blog, you can begin to promote this as being your success point, which makes you valuable to potential advertisers who want to promote with blogs like yours. So, as long as you continue increasing your value by sharing great and relevant content and promoting it effectively, your blog will grow.

Another great way to grow your blog is to consider spreading beyond your blog. Many bloggers will also establish their presence on social media so that when they are promoting their blog they are also growing their influencer accounts. This is especially common on Instagram where being an influencer can be especially valuable because you can profit from Instagram itself, too. This way, you can be earning money from sponsored social media posts *and* your blog, meaning that your entire brand expands, you become even more valuable, and your posts earn even more money for you. People who do this effectively can earn upward of $5,000 - $10,000+ per month from their blogs.

How Long It Will Take To See Profits

With blogging, your time to profitability naturally depends on how much you have invested and how much you are investing time wisely. If you start off smaller and invest consistent time every single day to writing for your blog and promoting it to other people, chances are you will start seeing a fairly consistent profit within 3-6 months, and that profit will continue steadily growing as you continue blogging.

CHAPTER 9

AFFILIATE MARKETING

Affiliate marketing is a great tool that you can use when it comes to creating a side hustle. If you already have a network established, affiliate marketing can begin earning you an income right away. Alternatively, you can develop a social media presence, a steady blog, or both and begin using this as a way to develop an audience to market to. Effectively building up an audience who is readily consuming your content is a great opportunity to ensure that you have plenty of people to market products to, which makes you a valuable asset to many different companies.

Why Affiliate Marketing Works

Affiliate marketing works by having you market products for companies to your already established audience. Many people find that their well-established audiences are readily willing to consume anything they offer because they feel confident that what that person markets is going to be positive and useful. As a result, any time their audience purchases something through their affiliate link, the affiliate is paid for a percentage of that income. Affiliate marketing works because consumers prefer word of mouth and social proof to prove that the products they are investing in are actually worth their investment. When people see that many other individuals are also having a positive experience with a brand, they are more likely to develop an interest in that brand and want to try it out for themselves. Even products that someone would normally never purchase will be purchased by an individual if someone they trust is excited enough about the products and swears by them. This is why so many "as seen on TV" products become fads: we see people on TV promoting them, one of our friends gives them a shot, and then suddenly everyone has them. Remember Eggies, Snuggies, and Sham Wows? All of these products blew up because of social proof, and the people who were affiliated with these products made a ton of money promoting them.

What You Need To Get Started

Getting started as an affiliate marketer is rather simple: you just need to have a strong network of people who trust in you to market your products to so that they are more likely to want to buy from you. You can get started with affiliate marketing by developing this network if you do not already have one so that you have an audience to market to, thus meaning that anyone willing to put in this legwork can get started. Most people who get involved in affiliate marketing will develop a strong online presence with their audience through Instagram, Facebook, Twitter, YouTube, or blogging. This way, they have a consistent platform to reach people and, because it is developed online, they can easily reach people who would have otherwise been impossible for them to reach through in person efforts. Once you have a trusting audience who is consistently engaging with your content you can go ahead and begin finding companies with affiliate programs that you can sign up with so that you can start marketing to your audience!

How To Get Started

After you have developed your strong network, all you need to do to get started with affiliate marketing is to find companies who have affiliate programs and who sell products relevant to you and your audience. Then, you sign up for these programs and receive a special link or code that your followers can use to purchase products through. Once you have those links, all you have to do is go ahead and start promoting their products to your audience. You want to make sure that all of your promotional posts are well-written and sound like you so that even though people know you are marketing to them it still feels authentic and genuine. Anything that does not sound like you will sound fake and may diminish your credibility online. Make sure that you always look at the rules on any platform that you are using, as well as for your locale, as many platforms and states have rules around how you can engage in affiliate marketing. It is important that you follow these rules so that your business stays legitimate and you can continue marketing to your audience and earning money this way for a long time.

How Successful You Will Be

Most affiliate marketers who place a strong emphasis on developing an audience and establishing credibility with their audience will earn upward of $2,500+ per month, with many falling in the $5,000 - $10,000+ range. If you want to establish credibility and really generate success you are going to always want to place your focus on developing an audience who trusts you and who likes you. This is typically done by having an audience who you continually work toward building a friendship with by regularly sharing your life with them and letting them see who you really are. The more you show that you are an authentic person, the more people will relate to you and the more they are going to want to trust in you and purchase what you share with them.

How to Scale Your Business

Scaling your affiliate marketing business will work much in the same way as scaling a blogging business. You can scale your affiliate marketing business by continually growing your audience and driving more traffic to your affiliate marketing links. When it comes to your affiliate marketing business, your value is perceived by the number of followers you have on social media and how engaged your followers are. Ideally, someone with a large audience that is also largely engaged is someone who is going to have more traffic coming through to their page, making them a more valuable asset. This way, if you choose to start an affiliate deal with someone, you know that you have enough people engaging with you that you should make a decent profit off of the deal. Likewise, the larger your audience grows and the more engaged they are, the more likely brands are going to start reaching out to you and promoting to you because they want to reach your audience. This means that the more time you spend refining your audience and growing it steadily, the more valuable you become and the more profits you are going to earn.

How Long It Will Take To See Profits

Because it is free to develop a network and grow your social media account, you can begin seeing profits in your affiliate marketing business right from your very first deal. The consistent profits will generally start rolling in between 3-6 months after you begin your affiliate marketing business and, for most, they will consistently reach above $1,000 per month within the first year of business. Of course, as with anything of this nature, the more you are committed to building your presence and developing trust with your audience, the more you are going to be growing online. This means that your credibility and value go up and your earnings will also go up. So, the more you focus on credibility and trust, the sooner you will see significant profits.

CHAPTER 10

MULTI-LEVEL MARKETING

Contrary to popular belief, multi-level marketing, and affiliate marketing are not one in the same. Although the work itself is the same, since you are promoting products to your network, multi-level marketing actually has the capacity to earn you a greater income because you are not putting so much work into keeping your audience growing. With multi-level marketing, there are far more ways to earn income and there are also opportunities for you to earn residual income that comes in each month regardless of whether or not you post anything. For that reason, getting into multi-level marketing may be more desirable to some people. However, multi-level marketing does come with the reputation of being a scam or something not worthy of peoples' investments, so you may have to put some work in getting beyond this belief system as you start developing your business.

Why Multi-Level Marketing Works

Multi-level marketing works because it provides you with the opportunity to grow a network that you profit off of, essentially. With multi-level marketing, you earn an income both from your customers who purchase from you and from people who join to sell products with you. If you build your network effectively, you could be earning upward of $100,000 per month from multi-level marketing. In fact, multi-level marketing has been said to create more millionaires than any other industry in the world. Multi-level marketing works because there are so many ways that you earn income from your business, and many of those ways are consistently earning for you even when you are not putting any work in. For example, if you grow a network of people who are running their businesses after recruiting through you, also known as a "down line," you can earn a percentage of their income, too. This is how many people become millionaires through this business model and retire without even having to work their multi-level marketing business anymore.

What You Need To Get Started

Multi-level marketing is a semi-passive business opportunity that can become completely passive if you work it enough in the beginning. In order to get started, all you need is a network of people that you can market to, which can easily be grown online if you want to have a larger reach within your audience. Then, you also need a company that you can join, someone who can recruit you, and a team who is going to help you achieve success. Other than that, you will need anywhere from $50 - $2,500 to purchase the starter kit for your company so that you can sign up as a marketer and have products that you can start promoting to your audience. Ideally, if you have never tried the company before you will purchase some basic products from your potential sponsor first so that you can give them a try and honestly endorse them to your audience.

How To Get Started

To get started with multi-level marketing, you have to consider what business is going to be most relevant to you and what you are going to get the most use out of. Finding the right industry that fits in with your lifestyle is a great opportunity to make sure that you are getting everything you want and need out of your company. It also ensures that it is easy for you to market the products because you are already likely to be using them on a regular basis in your life anyway, so now you are just swapping them out, promoting them, and earning an income from that. Once you have considered an industry that makes sense to you, you can go ahead and find a company that has a compensation plan that is going to earn you big profits. You want to have a company with a compensation plan that is easy to understand and that earns you plenty so that you can start earning money as soon as possible, and so that you can easily explain to other people how the earnings work, too. After you have found your company, you want to sign up with the biggest kit that you can afford and then go ahead and start marketing the products out of your starter kit!

How Successful You Will Be

Developing success with a multi-level marketing company all comes down to your mindset, which unfortunately is the failing point for many people. If you have a poor mindset where you already believe that multi-level marketing is a scam and that you are ripping people off or that you are not going to make money because "no one ever does," naturally you are not going to make any money with this opportunity. However, if you can surround yourself with positive and inspiring people and start focusing on how great the opportunity is and how people are already succeeding with it, you can generate massive success. The difference between the people who quit and the people who make $100,000+ per month is that the ones who make millions of dollars per year refused to listen to the crowd and went ahead anyway. As a result, they generated massive success and found themselves living as millionaires early on.

How to Scale Your Business

The key to scaling a multi-level marketing business is to keep talking about your company with people and offering it to people who might be interested. Make it easy for people to join you, show them how much fun you are having and how big your profits are, and have confidence in sharing your products. Show those people that this is going to be your opportunity to grow and that you are making plenty of money off of your business, regardless of what anyone is saying about you or your company. As your team starts to grow, put in the effort to educate them on how to market effectively and pass around high quality marketing skills that set you and your team apart from the crowd. The more you and your team grow beyond the status quo for the multi-level marketing industry, the more success you are going to have with your business.

How Long It Will Take To See Profits

Understanding the timeline for seeing profits with multi-level marketing can be tricky because it varies greatly. On one hand, you could sign up with a company for very little and start earning profits rapidly *if* you were consistently getting sales. However, most smaller business kits do not have the capacity to earn as many sales because you do not have as many products to show people and people do not take you quite as seriously. On the other hand, if you buy a $2,500+ kit you may take a while to see profits back because of the amount of your initial investment. However, people do realize that you are way more serious about it and that you must be in love with the products if you purchased that many. For that reason, your sweet spot for making fast profits likely lies in the medium range of $250-$1,000 starter kits. However, if you want to accumulate a larger amount of profits over time, you may be better to buy a kit in the $750-$2,500 range. The standard time period to start seeing consistent profits for a multi-level marketing company is 9-18 months, and it typically takes around 2-3 years to start earning over $50,000+ per month.

CHAPTER 11

YOUTUBE

YouTube is a great social media platform that can earn you a significant amount of profits if you leverage the platform correctly. Like blogging, YouTube has many ways for you to earn an income and it can be done by having a consistent stream of people watching your page. The more you spend time building your YouTube channel, the more income you are going to earn this way, so know that this can be a very lucrative income opportunity if you let it be. Believe it or not, YouTube was the original platform for influencers, and it still has a strong capacity to help people establish themselves as influencers on the internet. For that reason, it is a strong platform for people to start using if they want to earn a side income doing something fun and enjoyable.

Why YouTube Works

If you enjoy developing videos and speaking in front of a camera, YouTube can be an incredible business opportunity. Getting on YouTube and sharing videos about what you are doing or products that you are loving is a great opportunity for you to begin creating a presence for yourself and establishing credibility and trust with your audience. When people see you on camera, they have a greater likelihood of trusting in you because they feel as though you are talking directly to them, which helps them feel like you are being more personable and friendly. For many, this activates the part of their mind that feels connected to another human, making it easier for them to believe in you and in what you are saying. This is exactly why video marketing is taking off and so many people are seeing increased benefit from video marketing over any other marketing method. Once you have established this credible presence, you can make money on YouTube through monetizing your channel with advertisements, sharing sponsored videos, and promoting affiliate marketing products in your videos.

What You Need To Get Started

Getting started with YouTube can be a little more costly as you need to make sure that you have all of the right things to help you get started. If you want to get started as cheap as possible you can find a high quality camera within your budget, and maybe a tripod to prop your camera on. If you get started this way, your YouTube channel can cost as little as $600 to get started. It is important to make sure that you buy a camera that shoots in at least 1080p, however, as anything lower and your audience is not going to want to watch your videos. If you want to get started a little more high end and have a great channel from the start, you can purchase a nicer camera, a tripod, a ring light, and decent editing software like iMovie or Final Cut Pro, each of which is a great tool to use. These tools can cost you around $1,250 to get started, however, they will not need to be replaced or upgraded as soon so you can likely get away with these tools for much longer than you could a cheap camera and a cheap tripod. Either way, however, start with what fits your budget and go from there.

How To Get Started

Getting started on YouTube ultimately comes with making videos that are interesting and relevant and that show you off to your audience. You can use your expertise in a certain niche industry to educate your audience on various things or, if you would prefer, you can use your knack for comedy to make videos that are entertaining and interesting to your audience. Once you know the content that you want to create, all you have to do is set up your equipment and start filming. Then, afterward, you can edit your video and upload it to a YouTube channel. Ideally, you should create a YouTube channel that has a relevant name, attractive channel art, a profile picture, and a description that helps people know what you are all about. If you want to take your platform next level you can also include a channel trailer that welcomes people to your page as soon as they find it on desktop.

How Successful You Will Be

YouTube success depends on your ability to create high quality videos that are relevant while also being able to market them effectively to an audience who is going to watch your videos. If you get all three of these parts of your YouTube channel sorted out you can become highly successful, with many popular YouTube channels earning upward of $5,000 per month in their first two years in business. In your first year, you can expect to start earning upward of $1,000 per month in your first six months if you treat your channel as a business and not just a place to share videos. A great way to set yourself up for success is to follow other successful YouTube creators in your niche, and others in general, and do what you can to replicate what they are doing in terms of how they are creating and marketing content. The more clear you are with your marketing, the more effective your channel will grow and therefore the more you will stand to earn.

How to Scale Your Business

The best way to scale your YouTube business is to set yourself up for success right from the start. Choose a niche that has plenty of opportunities for you to promote as an affiliate, share sponsored videos, and get paid content out there. The more expandable your niche is, the more you are going to be able to grow into it and start taking advantage of all of the niche's opportunities because you will have set yourself up for success from day one. Once you have found that niche and started growing in it, all you need to do is go ahead and keep building up your audience so that you can increase your channel's traffic. Remember the more people who watch your videos, the more people that you have to market to which means that you also have a greater chance of earning a higher profit from your channel.

How Long It Will Take To See Profits

With YouTube, it can take a significant period of time to see profits if you are not fully educated in what you are doing. If you start your channel off poorly and do not begin by creating high quality videos with a clear purpose right from the start, you are going to find yourself taking 6-12 months or even longer to consistently make a profit off of your channel. If, however, you pretend that you are already wildly successful and you start making the highest quality videos that you can from day 1 and you promote them regularly, you can start earning a higher profit sooner. Some YouTube creators report having earned their profit in as early as month 3, and with a consistent profit rolling in by month 6. The more consistent that you can be with creating high quality content for your audience, the sooner you will begin seeing your profitable income.

CHAPTER 12

TURO

Turo is a car rental company whereby people who own their cars can rent their cars out to individuals who need a temporary car and earn money from it. This is an excellent opportunity for anyone who owns their own car and does not use it on a regular basis to rent out their car and receive extra income from that. Many people are using it as a way to earn an extra income on their secondary cars, or for people who are interested in renting out their primary car if they are not using it often to earn a profit, too.

Why Turo Works

Turo works because people are always interested in renting cars and, for the most part, renting from a person is cheaper and easier than renting from a business. Not only is it easier to get approved to rent these cars, but it is also easier for the payment, pick up, and drop off to be handled because it is being dealt with directly through the owner, and Turo. As a car owner, Turo works because you are being protected by a company who ensures that you and your vehicle are protected. This also means that you do not have to advertise your car for rent as you can simply put it on Turo and let their search engine based market place do the work for you. As a result, all you have to do is get your car on there and start earning bookings, which will earn you a profit from your vehicle.

What You Need To Get Started

Getting started with Turo is easy, all you need is a vehicle that you own and that has the right insurance for you to be using it as a rental car. Then, you can create a Turo account and upload your car with any information that is relevant to your car so that people can decide whether or not they want to rent it. After that, you simply wait for the rental offers to start coming in! If you have offered to drop off and pick up the car you will also need to have a plan in place to arrange this so that you can have your car delivered and received from the renter. Other than these few basic startup requirements, you can go ahead and start renting your car on Turo!

How To Get Started

Before you start renting out your car it is important that you talk to your insurance company and get the proper insurance on your car for business use. Not having the right insurance on your car can cause Turo to deny your car being able to be rented out, and it can cause serious liabilities for you if someone rents out your car and gets into an accident or otherwise causes trouble with it. In some cases, it can cause your insurer to deny you insurance in the future because they now see you as high risk and they do not want to offer you insurance. Once you have the right insurance on, you will need to go to Turo's website and set up an account as someone who owns a vehicle that they are ready to rent out. From there,

Turo will walk you through the process of setting up your account and getting your car listed on their platform. They will also ensure that you know of any guidelines or requirements as a vehicle owner to be working with them, and it is important that you pay attention. Remember, this is a business and you are renting out your car so you want to be professional and thorough about the entire process to ensure that you earn a profit without accidentally running into liability issues due to a lack of thoroughness.

How Successful You Will Be

Depending on how often your car is available and how much you are able to charge per day, you can easily start earning $1,000+ per month on Turo. Your maximum earnable income on this platform will ultimately depend on how nice your car is, how well priced it is compared to other similar vehicles, and how frequently you can keep your vehicle rented out for. The more your vehicle is rented, obviously, the more you will earn money from this service.

How to Scale Your Business

Scaling your Turo business can either be done by making your car more readily available or purchasing and renting out a second car if you find that you are earning enough to make this a wise move. Not everyone will find that this makes sense for them, however, so for many people, they simply earn an additional income off of their car and that is it. Still, if you wanted to, you could go ahead and start purchasing nicer cars and renting them out consistently to earn a profit. It all depends on how much you are making per month and if it seems feasible to purchase another car or not.

How Long It Will Take To See Profits

With Turo, you can begin seeing profits as early as your first month, so long as your car gets rented out. Since most cars have fairly consistent rental rates, you can expect to be seeing your $1,000+ income from Turo in as little as 3-6 months, as long as you keep your car readily available and keep your ratings up. At the end of each rental period, the renter has the opportunity to rate you and your car and if these ratings stay high your car is more likely to be rented out. If, however, these ratings go down, you may make it hard to get your car rented out again which can mean that you are going to lose your opportunity to earn a profit from Turo.

CHAPTER 13

AIRBNB

Airbnb is like Turo except for homes. Many people who have vacation homes, or who have larger homes where they can afford to rent out a room or a private suite in their home use Airbnb as an opportunity to earn money from their home. Keeping your home rented out this way is a great opportunity to start earning an income on space that you are not using without having to have it permanently rented out. Many property owners prefer this because they can simply make the property unavailable to be rented any time they want to use the property and they can rent it out anytime they are not using the property for an income. This makes the property more flexible because it can be used by both the home owner and vacationers, rather than having it permanently rented out and unavailable to be used by the home owner.

Why Airbnb Works

Airbnb works because people are always looking for a place to stay when they are travelling and for many staying in an Airbnb feels way more personable and comfortable than staying in a hotel. Hotels can be very cold and unwelcoming and while

51

they have room service and built-in amenities like pools and gyms, they can also be uncomfortable. Often, the rooms are small, the bathrooms are not too nice, and they can feel cramped. Airbnb vacation homes, however, can feel far more comfortable and accommodating because they are true homes. Most times, the owner decorates it like a home and it feels comfortable and cozy and far more accommodating for guests. Many Airbnb properties also have direct access to outside which means that they can be enjoyed by people who are not interested in being cramped in tiny rooms with very little space to do anything. Because of how comfortable they can be, Airbnb can be a great opportunity for vacationers to feel more at ease during their travels, which means that home owners have a great opportunity to rent to these interested vacationers.

What You Need To Get Started

In order to get started with Airbnb, you are going to need to have a property that you can rent out and permission to rent out part of your property if you are not the direct owner of that property. Not every land owner will be okay with their renters renting out parts of the property to vacationers, so make sure that you get an agreement in writing if your land owner says it is okay to avoid legal troubles in the future. Otherwise, if you are a land owner yourself then you are in the clear. However, you may need to check your local bylaws as not all locales allow Airbnb type rentals due to poor economies or housing crisis for people who already live in the area. As long as you are legally in the clear, you can go ahead and upgrade your home insurance to accommodate for Airbnb renters and then begin renting out your property!

How To Get Started

To get started with Airbnb you are going to need to create an account on Airbnb that is designed for property owners. Your profile is going to require you to have your own personal profile that will be attached to your rentals, as this is how Airbnb promotes each property: by also promoting the property owner. This gives each property a more personal feel, as well as gives renters an idea of who they will be renting from so that they feel more comfortable with staying with you or on your property. After making your personal profile, you will go ahead and make a listing for each of the properties that you have available to be rented. Each property will need a name, a description, high quality photographs, and information about how it can be rented and what the rules are for anyone who stays on your property. Once all of this is set up, all you have to do is leave your listing up and let Airbnb promote your property in searches until someone decides to rent your property from them!

How Successful You Will Be

Airbnb has been known to help people make a massive amount of income off of their property. The thing about Airbnb is that profits can shift from month to month as seasons shift and travelers are either visiting frequently or not as much because the traveling season is over. That being said, if you can get a nice property that is well-priced and enjoyable to stay at, you could earn as much as $10,000 per month during peak season. Despite the months fluctuating, Airbnb is known for having nearly 50% of all of their hosts earning more than $500 per month, which makes it an excellent platform for you to get on and earn money with.

How to Scale Your Business

Scaling your Airbnb business will work if you either purchase more property to rent or you have more space that you can make available. Alternatively, increasing your amount of availability and keeping your host rating high so that people know that you are a great place to stay at is another way that you can scale your business. The more people know about you and see you as having the best property with the best experience, the more people are going to want to stay with you, which will keep you booked up more frequently. This way, if having more property or more time availability is not feasible, then at least you are maximizing what you already have and earning as much as you can off of your property.

How Long It Will Take To See Profits

With Airbnb, the platform itself dramatically reduces the amount of time it takes to see rental profits from vacation properties. It also reduces the amount of time that it takes to make your money back since you are not renting per month but instead per night, which means that you are actually earning 5-20% more on your property, assuming that you can keep it booked at least 80% of the time. Although you will start earning an income from the property right away, it is technically not considered profitable until the property is paid off completely. The average amount of time it takes for home owners to completely pay off their homes with Airbnb rentals is approximately 154 months or 12 years, as opposed to the average 256 months or 21.5 years when you rent out your property the traditional way. This means that most properties can be paid off in half the time with Airbnb than with traditional rentals, which is a great opportunity for people who have rental properties to get into profits faster.

CHAPTER 14

UBER/LYFT

Uber and Lyft are two different companies where people can offer to provide transportation services to other people. Essentially, if you become an Uber driver or a Lyft driver, you become a personal taxi service to customers on the Uber or Lyft platforms. Becoming an Uber driver or a Lyft driver in modern days can be a great opportunity to earn cash in your spare time as you simply offer taxi services to people who need rides. Many people earn a great profit off of this platform and because you are the one offering the services, you also get to create your own hours which means that you can easily fit this work in around what you are already doing. That being said, Uber drivers and Lyft drivers are putting in work to make their money, so this is considered linear income as opposed to passive or semi-passive income.

Why Uber and Lyft Work

Uber and Lyft work because, to put it simply, there are typically more drivers available than taxi drivers, the drivers tend to be more personable, and it is insanely easy. Instead of having to search for a taxi company's number and pay their high rates to get anywhere, people can get on the Uber app or the Lyft app and hire a driver to come directly to their location and pick them up so that they can get to their next location. Not only is it typically cheaper, but you can also take advantage of accommodations like smaller or larger vehicles depending on the number of travelers and even car seats if you have children. Plus, Uber drivers and Lyft drivers often want to put in extra effort for positive feedback so that they are more likely to get higher tips and increased bookings, so they will often do things to make your drive more enjoyable. Some of these things include offering candies, gum, inexpensive umbrellas, and even the opportunity to go through a drive thru on your way somewhere in case you wanted coffee or a meal. Of course, you will pay for your own drive thru, but the idea that they will stop for you is great.

What You Need To Get Started

Getting started as an Uber driver or a Lyft driver first requires you to apply to become a driver. Each company has their own qualifications required to become a driver, but typically you need to have a clean driver's abstract, a clean criminal record and be able to pass their basic driving test to prove that you are a safe driver. After that, you need to get the proper insurance for your vehicle so that it can be used as a work vehicle, as well as get your vehicle ready for being used as a taxi. As long as you can meet all of these qualifications, you can begin driving as an Uber driver or a Lyft driver in relatively minimal timing.

How To Get Started

If you want to get started as an Uber driver or a Lyft driver, you must first decide what platform you want to use and then look into whether or not that platform is available in your area. These two platforms are not available in every community, so it is important that you first look into this before getting into the process of getting everything else set up. Once you know that your community has either platform, you can go ahead and sign up on their website as a potential driver. You will be guided to fill out and application and shown how you can provide certain pieces of relevant documentation so that you can prove that you will not be a liability to their company. After you have completed all of this, you will need to call your insurance company and get your car insured for the proper insurance to be used as a business vehicle. You may also need to update your registration so that your vehicle is registered properly as well. Your local registry office should be able to provide you with information on how this can all be changed so that your vehicle can legally be used as a business vehicle. It is important that you do this as not having it done can put you personally at risk of major fines as well as major losses should anything go wrong. Once you have passed all of the application processes and adjusted your registration and insurance, you can go ahead and create your Uber or Lyft profile. Then, all you need to do is "respond" to potential jobs when you have extra time to make money and drive around, and start driving people to their destinations!

How Successful You Will Be

Uber drivers are said to take home $25 per hour whereas Lyft drivers are said to take home $35 per hour. That being said,

Uber takes 25% of each fare for their platform fees and Lyft takes 20% of each fare. If you are choosing which one to work with, ideally you should aim to work with Lyft if you want to make more since they pay more and take less from each fare. In addition to your hourly wages, you can also earn tips from your clients, which means that you have the capacity to earn even more. How much you will earn per month depends on how much you are available to drive, so the more you drive the more you will earn. That being said, if you could contribute just 12 hours of driving per week to your Uber business you could be earning $960 per month before tips, and if you devoted the same amount to Lyft you could be earning $1,400 per month before tips. That is not a lot of extra hours to devote to earn such an incredible income from driving around!

How to Scale Your Business

Scaling your Uber or Lyft business will ultimately come from providing more hours to driving, and keeping your ratings high. The better your ratings are, the more people are going to want to book with you because the more you are doing to make their ride comfortable and enjoyable. This also means that you are more trustworthy because you have higher ratings, therefore meaning that people are going to be more likely to choose you over someone with lower ratings. Think about it: if you were about to get in the car with someone, would you want someone with a 4.5 star rating or higher or someone with a 2-4 star rating? Probably the higher rating, because this person is more likely to be a safe driver who can get you from point A to point B while also making your drive comfortable and enjoyable.

How Long It Will Take To See Profits

Exactly when you start earning profits somewhat depends on whether or not you own your car outright and how much time you are devoting to your business. Technically, if you do not own your car outright and you are still making payments on it, it will take longer for you to become profitable because you are still paying for your vehicle. However, if you own your vehicle outright, you can start seeing profits as early as that month, as long as you are driving regularly.

CHAPTER 15

SKIP THE DISHES OR UBER EATS

Skip the Dishes and Uber Eats are similar to Uber or Lyft, except that instead of driving people around you drive food around. For many people, this feels like a safer or more ideal option as they are willing to drive but feel uncomfortable having strangers in their car. If you would like to make money driving but do not want to run the risk of having potentially rude or ill people driving with you, or perhaps you are simply anxious or do not like being around other people much, this is a great alternative. While Skip the Dishes and Uber Eats will not earn you as much as Uber or Lyft would, they will still earn you a decent side income if you are willing to do enough work in your spare time.

Why Skip The Dishes and Uber Eats Works

Skip the Dishes and Uber Eats are two highly popular food delivery services that are highly favored by locals who are interested in ordering from restaurants but do not want to dine in or go pick up takeout. Thanks to these two delivery services, restaurants that never provided delivery in the past now provide delivery on many of people's favorite dishes. This means that people who previously refrained from eating at certain restaurants are now able to get food from there because they can have it delivered directly to their house. Now, rather than having to choose between Pizza or Chinese Food, people can choose between anything that is offered in their local areas, such as raw vegan food, Indian food, and even bakery foods that are now being delivered.

As a driver, driving for Skip the Dishes and Uber Eats gives you the opportunity to cash in on this lucrative deal as well, earning money for each delivery that you make. Delivery drivers are paid per delivery, as well as tips from customers, which means that they are able to earn a fair amount from each trip they make. If you want to get involved in driving action but do not want to rent out your car or have people travelling with you around the city, Skip the Dishes or Uber Eats are two great alternatives.

What You Need To Get Started

To get started with your Skip the Dishes or Uber Eats driving business, you are going to need to have a reliable car, the right insurance for your car, and an account with the company that allows you to drive on their behalf. The courier apps for both Skip the Dishes and Uber Eats are different than the customer apps, and they are used for helping you see where you need to go and what you need to pick up. You will need the courier app so that you can gain access to your account, book shifts, "clock in" and "clock out," and gain access to your delivery information. In addition to that, you will need a working cellphone that the dispatchers can contact so that they can get ahold of you and let you know where to go to pick up your next order. As long as you have these things in place, the up-front cost for getting started is actually free.

How To Get Started

To get started as a delivery driver for either Skip the Dishes or Uber Eats, you are going to need to go to the website of that company and fill out an application to become a delivery driver. The application is relatively short and does not take long to be approved. Once it has been, you will need to call your insurance agent for your vehicle and upgrade your insurance to include vehicle insurance. This is necessary because if you get in an accident with your vehicle and it is discovered that you are driving for business without the proper insurance, your insurance agent has the right to waive your insurance altogether, which can place a huge liability on you. After your application has been approved and your car insurance has been adjusted, all you have to do is download the courier app and begin applying for shifts. According to existing drivers, Uber Eats may be better if you are the type of person who last minute decides to cancel a shift because Skip the Dishes makes it more challenging for you to skip shifts without quitting your job altogether, and becoming non-rehirable. When your shifts are approved, all you have to do is wait for a dispatcher to call you and begin running the orders that you are given!

How Successful You Will Be

People who drive on a consistent part time schedule with either Skip the Dishes or Uber Eats report to regularly earn between $500 and $2000 per month from their driving. To give you an exact dollar value, most people report earning between $8-$12 per hour plus tips and after gas expenses with Skip the Dishes or $7.50 - $11 per hour plus tips and after gas expenses with Uber Eats.

Exactly how much you will earn depends on how much time you are willing to put into your driving, so that will heavily determine the amount that you earn. As well, if people choose to tip you more, you can earn more through these tips. As a general rule of thumb, driving on a Friday or a Saturday during lunch hour rush and dinner hour rush is the best time to get tips from people, and in many cases, they will tip you on the app and then also tip you cash at the door. This is a great opportunity to earn even more from your driving. Avoid working on Mondays and Tuesdays, as these tend to be the worst days for tips. If you really want to earn the most, always drive between lunch hour rushes and dinner hour rushes, as these are going to be the times when you have more people ordering, meaning that you will have more to do. The more deliveries you are driving, the more cash you earn!

How To Scale Your Business

Unless you want to put more hours into driving, there really is no way to scale your Skip the Dishes or Uber Eats businesses. These are just excellent side hustles for anyone who has extra time and enjoys driving, as it gives you an opportunity to earn some extra cash while also exploring your city. Many drivers report that they love the opportunity to see more of their city, as they are generally not exposed to the areas of the city that they discover when driving for Skip the Dishes or Uber Eats. Although this has nothing to do with profitability or earnings, it can be a nice little benefit to anyone who enjoys exploring and wants to earn some money while doing it.

How Long It Will Take To See Profits

With Skip the Dishes or Uber Eats, profits can generally be seen right from your very first trip, unless of course, you are still making payments on your car loan. In this case, technically profits are earned after your car loan is paid off. That being said, many people find that working part time for Skip the Dishes or Uber Eats is a great opportunity to earn extra income to pay for their monthly auto loan, which makes it easier for them to continue having the money to pay for said loan. This way, rather than coming out of their monthly earnings, their auto loan comes back from the car itself. This can be an intelligent way to pay your loan, or to pay it off faster if you put your entire profits toward your car loan!

CHAPTER 16

ATM

ATM machines are actually a great way to earn money. Many people purchase ATM machines and place them around their towns and earn money every single time someone does a transaction through the machine. For some people, this is a lucrative business opportunity that can help them earn more. You could even add one to another side hustle, like a laundromat, and significantly increase your earnings from that side hustle. There are many ways that an ATM can be incorporated into your side hustle to help you earn some cash without having to do anything for it.

Why ATM Works

ATM machines are a great opportunity to earn a profit because, quite simply, many people are going to need cash at one time or another and if they use your ATM machine you get paid for it. Every single time a transaction is processed through your machine you can earn anywhere from $1.50 to $5.00 per transaction, which adds up quickly if you have a machine that is well-placed. Common places for ATMs include gas stations or convenience stores, event halls, casinos, and anywhere else where an ATM may frequently be used. These are a great low-maintenance semi-passive income opportunity for anyone who wants to earn cash without having to do much to make it happen. In fact, most businesses who will benefit from having one will incorporate one into their business to ensure that they themselves are earning, even more, thus maximizing their earnings overall.

What You Need To Get Started

Getting started with an ATM business really only requires one thing: an ATM machine. Once you have your own ATM machine all you need to do is find a place to put it and then set it up. If you do not own your own place of business where you can put an ATM machine, you can always call around to local businesses to offer them to place your machine there so that you can earn an income. Typically, a business will say yes as long as they earn a percentage of your earnings to ensure that they are also being compensated for it. Typically, they will ask for anywhere from 10-40% of your earnings, which means that you would be giving them $0.25 to $1.00 per standard $2.50 transaction fee.

How To Get Started

The first thing you need to do is buy an ATM machine so that you have one that can start earning you money. You could buy a used machine, but ideally, you should buy a new one so that it is compatible with the latest technology and comes with a warranty, which means that you can earn more transactions and stay protected against malfunction or damage. The machine will likely run you anywhere from $2,000 - $8,000. If you have more to invest, you can always buy more than one machine so that you can begin earning on multiple locations at once. In addition to owning the machine, you are also going to need to learn how it works so that you can set it up, set up the transaction fee, and learn how to keep it stocked. When it is properly functioning and delivering cash to recipients, you are going to be earning. When it is out of funds or not functioning properly, you are not going to be earning anything. Aside from that, you are going to need to make a deal with a local business to place your machine unless you have a place that you can put it yourself. If you are putting it in someone else's place of business, make sure that you keep the keys and the tools to access it, and that the business owner signs a document agreeing that it is yours. Your agreement should also outline how much you are going to give them per month to have your ATM placed so that you are both protected.

How Successful You Will Be

How many machines you have and how frequently they are being used ultimately plays into how much you are going to earn from your ATM business, but the average business will make $300 - $800+ per month per machine depending on where the location is. If you have your machine located in a favorable place that has it being used regularly, you can make closer to $800. If you have two machines located in favorable places, you can make upward of $1,600, and so forth. The things that will impact your success include how frequently it is being used, where it is located, and what the note capacity of your ATM machine is. The more money your machine can hold, and the more frequently it is stocked, the more you are going to earn in the long run, as this means that it can run several transactions before running out of cash. It is a good idea to regularly check on your machines so that you can keep them stocked, which will ensure that they are always in working order and that you can earn more from them.

How to Scale Your Business

The easiest way to scale your ATM business is to continually buy new machines and place them in areas where they are going to be used on a consistent basis. Favor businesses that have low vendor fees and high traffic so that you are earning consistent transactions and not having to give so much of your profits away to the vendors. As well, try and keep your machines centrally located so that it is easier for you to get to each machine to stock it. The more machines you can buy and maintain, the more you are going to earn through your business, so ultimately this is the best way for you to grow your ATM business. The average person with 4 ATM machines can earn anywhere from $1,200 to $3,200+ per month, making it an excellent opportunity to earn an additional income without having to do too much to keep it going.

How Long It Will Take To See Profits

The average ATM business will begin to see profits within about 12 months. Depending on how much you have spent on the machine and what you are paying per transaction to your vendor, this timespan can fluctuate. However, in order to get the best profits from your business, you are going to need to expect to keep your business going for about 12 months before you break even and begin profiting. After that, your machine will be paid back and you will start earning your $300 - $800+ per month with your ATM business.

CHAPTER 17

REAL ESTATE AGENT

Becoming a real estate agent is a linear income, however, because you are your own boss you can fit it around your existing schedule and start earning an income through real estate sales. As a real estate agent, you can decide when you are going to show homes, how many you are going to show, and what hours you are going to work. You get to set your own hours and determine your own appointments and, as such, you can easily fit this business around any other work you are already doing. Plus, real estate agents can make a significant amount of money, making this a rather lucrative side hustle if you are looking to earn a decent wage.

Why Becoming A Real Estate Agent Works

Real estate is always up, either for sale or to be bought. Regardless of whether it is a buyer's market or a seller's market, a real estate agent can earn money from their involvement in the process. Being a part time real estate agent means that you can set your own hours and do the amount of work that you want to do and nothing more. Even though you will work with a brokerage, as required by law, you are still considered self-employed which means that you are responsible for all of the work that you do. The more that you keep yourself working in your down hours, the more you are going to earn, which means that you can make a decent wage as a real estate agent.

What You Need To Get Started

Getting started as a real estate agent first requires you to become licensed as one, which requires you to go through an educational program and then pass exams and pay for your licensing fees. Your classes and exams can cost anywhere from $4,000 to $8,000 depending on where you live and what the requirements are. You also have to work with a brokerage which includes brokerage fees, which can range anywhere from 1-3% of the cost of the home you sell, as well as annual fees which can be anywhere from $1,000 to $12,000 per year. Once you have your licensing and have signed up to work with a brokerage, you need to begin finding clients to work with you so that you can list and sell homes. Most real estate agents need to do their own groundwork for finding homes to sell and finding buyers to sell to, though some brokerages will help you with advertising features built into your brokerage fee. You will need to explore what options are available to you to ensure that you are getting out in front of potential clients so that you can earn an income through your real estate agent side hustle.

How To Get Started

Getting started as a real estate agent first requires you to pass your exams. If you have not yet passed them, your first order of business is going to be looking into the legal requirements for real estate agents in your state and then meeting those requirements. Any real estate agent who attempts to get into the business without these basic legal requirements met will not be accepted by any legitimate brokerage, which means that you will not be able to get into the business of buying and selling homes. After you have passed your exams you need to find a brokerage to work through, which is a legal requirement. Brokerages are like agencies that real estate agents go through so that they can legally buy and sell land between their clients. Virtually every state requires you to work with a brokerage, so you are going to need to find one that fits your needs that you can work with before you get started. Once you have, all you have to do is begin marketing yourself in your local area as a real estate agent so that you can begin finding clients to buy and sell for. Many new real estate agents will offer referral rewards of $100 - $1,000 to anyone who sends business their way so long as those clients go through with buying or selling, as this offers an incentive for people to spread their name around. Once they grow larger in size, they often stop offering these referral rewards as they are now more well-known and can continue growing off of the existing word of mouth that they already have.

How Successful You Will Be

Real estate agents can make anywhere from $30,000 - $56,000 per year after brokerage and licensing fees if they are working 10-30 hours per week selling homes. As long as you continue advertising and working your business on a regular basis you can make an additional $30,000 - $56,000 per year on top of what you already make as a real estate agent. This number will fluctuate depending on what your brokerage fees actually are, how much you are investing in advertising, and how often you are actually buying and selling homes. The quicker you can buy and sell your home, the faster you can turn profits which means the more you will earn in the long run.

How to Scale Your Business

Scaling your real estate agent business can be done by becoming well known for what you do and having a lot of referrals sent your way. The more homes you are buying and selling for, the more you are going to earn in the long run. You can maximize your earnings by keeping your client roster full which means that you earn way more per year through your real estate business. If you find that you like selling real estate or that you prefer it to what you are already doing, you can always start selling real estate full time and begin earning $100,000 - $125,000+ per year from your business. How you decide to grow and how much you decide to grow ultimately depends on you and what you are looking for so that you can earn what is right for you.

How Long It Will Take To See Profits

Because of how costly it is to get into real estate, with exams, licensing fees, and brokerage fees, it can take about 4-6 months to break even in your business if you are working extremely part time hours (10-15 hours per week.) After that, you will be earning profits from every sale that you make through your business. You can make profits sooner, in as little as 2-3 months, if you start selling properties right away and you are putting in more hours per month. That being said, it can take some time to get the ball rolling as many people hire real estate agents by word of mouth and reviews which means that it may take some time for you to get your credibility established in your business. If you already have a decent network to reach out into, however, you can shorten the amount of time it takes you and get into sales quickly.

CHAPTER 18

FREELANCE

There are many different types of freelance work that you can get into, each of which can offer you the opportunity to start earning a side income. Freelancing work refers to any type of work that is typically done as a one-time deal with clients who are in need of an extra helping hand here and there. There are hundreds of freelance services that you can offer to help you earn extra money and, based on the nature of this work, you can set your own hours and work at your own pace. You also get to set your own wages which means that you can earn a great income through freelancing. Many people turn to freelancing as an opportunity to engage in their favorite hobbies or skills and earn some cash from it so that they can both have fun and earn an income simultaneously. This can be a great opportunity to make cash doing what you love, and potentially even lead into full time work if you set it up properly and find that you enjoy it enough.

Why Freelancing Works

Freelance works because people are always in need of additional services to be completed, regardless of what those services are. From the odd writing gig here and there to creative services like designing art or video editing, there are many different skills that can be turned into freelance work and used as an opportunity to earn an income. Many freelancers will offer multiple different skillsets to maximize their potential for working with a client so that they can receive a more significant income. The more you put your services out there and get to work, the more you are going to earn as a freelancer.

Types of Freelancing Work You Can Do

There are many different types of freelance work that you can do, depending on what you have as a skillset. The key here is to ensure that anything you offer to do for others is something that you are actually capable of doing so that people know that they can trust you and the services that you are offering. The more you can establish credibility and keep your ratings up, the more you are going to earn through freelance work, so this is important. Never list a skill that you do not have as this can lead to you getting poor reviews and losing credibility, ultimately diminishing your ability to earn an income as a freelancer over time.

To help you get an idea of what types of freelance work you can do, some common freelance gigs include things like:

- Web development and web designing
- Freelance writing and copywriting
- Creative design services (i.e. creating power points)
- Sales and marketing services (i.e. lead generation services)

- Graphic design
- Mobile app development
- Search engine optimization services (i.e. SEO and SEM)
- Branding and public relations services
- Admin support or admin assistance
- 3D modelling
- Game development
- Translation services
- Web research services
- Legal services
- Transcription services
- Writing articles or blog posts
- Customer service
- Social media coordinator
- Social media community manager (i.e. Facebook group admin)
- Logo design and logo illustration
- Audio and video production
- Data entry jobs
- Human resource management services
- Architecture services

Each of these services does require some degree of skill or background to ensure that you are capable of doing it, yet this is a rather diverse list which means that you are likely to have skills in one or more areas. Offering your services in one or more of these areas can be a great opportunity for you to offer freelance services and earn money as a result.

What You Need To Get Started

Getting started as a freelancer first requires you to have a skill that you are capable of monetizing so that you have something of value to offer to potential clients. If you already have a skill you do not need to worry about paying to educate yourself on said skill or teaching yourself how to do it, instead you can just begin offering it. Beyond having a skill, you need to market your skill to an audience of people so that you have the opportunity to monetize that skill. If you already have an audience that you can market to, such as a healthy social media audience, you can always begin by marketing to that part of your audience. Alternatively, you can use a platform like Upwork or Fiverr to get your services out to people who may be interested in working with you. Both of these platforms are like ready-made market places for freelancers to post their services and begin earning funds from people who are interested in working with you. That being said, platforms like Upwork and Fiverr do have more competitive market places and you have to pay the platform per gig that you do so that you can continue using their platform. However, if you are turning enough gigs around you can still earn an excellent profit this way.

How To Get Started

The best way to get started as a freelancer is to decide that you want to become one and then determine your marketing plan. Ideally, you should be actively marketing in one way or another so that you are getting your name out there and increasing your chances of getting discovered and earning a profit. If you are on a platform like Fiverr or Upwork, make sure that you create a solid advertisement for your services and then that you link those services to your social media accounts so that you can tap into your existing network, too. When people do begin to hire you, make sure that you do an excellent job and that you encourage them to leave a review on your profile so that people can see that you are a reliable person to hire. As you start to get jobs, make sure that you allot a reasonable amount of time each week toward completing your jobs so that you are getting them done in a timely manner and earning profits as a result. Pay close attention to detail as the better your services are the better your reviews will be, which means the more jobs you will get and the more you can charge per job in the long run.

How Successful You Will Be

Freelancers can make anywhere from an extra $500 a month to an extra $5,000+ per month, depending on how much they are charging and how much work they are doing per month. You can improve your odds of being successful by offering a wider range of services and keeping your services reasonably priced and with high ratings from people who do purchase from you. The better your ratings are and the more you are earning per job, the better your income from freelancing is going to be. If you find that you have a consistent income coming in this way and that you prefer it, you may even consider starting up your own freelancing agency so that you are acquiring clients through your own brand and you are no longer paying fees to other agencies. This way, you put the funds directly into your own pocket and you are earning a significant amount from your freelancing work.

How to Scale Your Business

Scaling your freelancing business can be done by charging more per job as you increase your credibility and become known for doing great work. The more you are known for being good at what you do, the more you can charge as your work is proven in value which makes you worth more. Aside from gradually increasing your prices, you can also do your best to keep your working hours full so that you are earning as much as you possibly can through your freelancing work. The more you are booked, and the more hours you can put toward your work, the more you are going to earn.

Another thing that some freelancers will do as they begin to book up is hiring other freelancers to work for them. If you choose to grow this way, you will be responsible for marketing to your audience and bringing on new clients and then designating certain freelancers to certain jobs. This way, you receive the money from the client and then you pay the money to the freelancer while keeping a percentage of what is paid. This can be a great way to capitalize on overflow if you have more clients than you can reasonably handle, meaning that you can scale your business and earn even more without having to do too much more work.

How Long It Will Take To See Profits

As a freelancer, you can typically see profits immediately since it rarely costs you anything to get started. If you start paying marketing fees or you pay to use a platform to market your services on, it may take you a month or two to break even, although this is rarely the case. Most freelancers start earning as much as $200 - $1,000 in their first month in business and then go on to earn upward of $1,000 per month the longer they do it. Many freelancers will even earn upward of $1,000 - $3,000 per month right from the first month, depending on how valuable their services are and how much time they have to devote to it. The more time you have, the better.

CHAPTER 19

VIRTUAL ASSISTANT

Becoming a virtual assistant means that you are working remotely for businesses, offering them services similar to that of an assistant. Virtual assistants generally cover various tasks for businesses ranging from responding to emails to setting up sales pages or creating autoresponders, and various other tasks. There are many things that virtual assistants can do for a company, although you are not required to be able to do everything to become one. As long as you have a healthy range of skills that can be of assistance to a personal brand or a business, you can earn a fairly decent profit as a virtual assistant. With more and more businesses going online and entrepreneurs rising in the online community, being a freelancer is becoming more and more lucrative, making this an excellent business opportunity for people who want to make some extra cash.

Why Being a Virtual Assistant Works

Being a virtual assistant is a great opportunity for you to earn an additional income while being able to decide on your own schedule and work around your existing obligations. If you are a virtual assistant, you have the opportunity to determine when you are going to work and how many people you are going to work for. The best part of working as a virtual assistant is that you are not generally required to work for specific hours, but instead, you are working within specific deadlines, which means that as long as you can allot enough time toward a project before the deadline is up you can go ahead and start working. This means that it does not matter if you work in the morning, in the afternoon, in the night, or even in the middle of the night, so truly you can work virtual assistant work around virtually everything.

Becoming a virtual assistant is an excellent opportunity for many people to make money from their computer as it is something that can be done at any time of the day and from any location. Since you are working remotely, as long as you have access to the internet you have the ability to make money as a freelancer. Many virtual assistants work by having just one or two live calls with their clients per month to ensure that they know what work needs to be done, followed by email support that ensures that they are staying on the same page as their clients. This means that you do not even have to worry about scheduling many specific sessions to speak with people live because most of what you do is remote and behind the scenes.

What You Need To Get Started

To get started as a virtual assistant, you really only need two things: skills, and clientele. You can become a virtual assistant by learning how to complete skills that are desirable or relevant to a specific industry or business model and then begin marketing your skills to businesses who exist in that model. A common type of person to become an assistant to is an online coach of sorts, such as life coaches or business coaches, as these are typically individuals who like to outsource their assistant work so that they can go ahead and focus on coaching clients. As a virtual assistant to a coach, to give you an example, some skills you might have included being able to respond to emails, set up automated newsletter style emails to send out to their email list, creating autoresponders on their social media accounts, scheduling social media posts, and more. These types of skills are things that allow you to do the work that a coach might not want to do but still needs to get done so that they are regularly engaging with their audience.

Once you have skills that people want, you need to start marketing to your audience. As a virtual assistant, it is typically easier for you to get into your existing network of business folks and start offering your services. Many virtual assistants will grow a network of business folk online and then start marketing their services on their platforms so that they can get discovered by the people who would be most likely to hire them. By getting in front of your audience you can easily start getting hired by people who already know you and trust you, which will allow you to earn a greater income from your business.

Skills that Virtual Assistants Have

There are two types of virtual assistants that exist: general virtual assistants (GVA's) and specialized virtual assistants who are great at a limited number of tasks. If you want to make it easier for people to hire you, being a general virtual assistant means that you can do more for a business which means that more smaller businesses will be likely to hire you. That being said, being a specialized virtual assistant means that you can charge more per gig because you are specialized with what you do and you are able to do more in a certain area of business. Some larger companies will hire special virtual assistants to do specific work because they can do higher quality of work in that area, which in turn earns the business more money. You can choose to do whichever suits what you can offer most, but make sure that whatever you offer is accurate to what you can do. The last thing you want to do is be hired by a company who expects that you can do justice to the work they need done, only to find that you are really not that good at it and they are left disappointed. Not only does that feel crummy, but it also diminishes your credibility and makes it harder for you to book gigs in the future.

To give you an idea of what skills you can offer as a virtual assistant, below are 25 different things that virtual assistants do for their clients. This list is designed to be inclusive of skills for a general virtual assistant, and even so not every single general virtual assistant needs to be offering all of these services. Still, the more that you can offer if you go this route, the more valuable you are to a company and the more work you will have to do. If you are only good at one or two things, however, consider marketing yourself as a specialized virtual assistant and charging more as this is your specialty.

The 25 skills that virtual assistants may be required to have include:

- Being able to manage emails, file them away in different email folders, and filter through the ones that are important

- Set up autoresponders or scheduled emailed newsletters on platforms like Aweber or Mailchimp
- Book appointments with clients using the company's scheduler
- Following up with clients with reminder emails for upcoming appointments and thank you letters following appointments
- Light receptionist duties, such as answering calls or taking virtual meetings on behalf of the company
- Managing the company's calendar by inputting availability and scheduling bookings or appointments into the calendar for them
- Managing the company's files by keeping documents organized on platforms like Drop Box or Google Drive
- Building databases such as email or contact lists
- Researching topics for things like blog posts, social media posts, or email newsletters
- Running personal errands, such as purchasing gifts for loved ones through online platforms like Amazon
- Booking hotels and flights for the company's upcoming trips
- Transcription work, such as transcribing voicemails, videos, audios, or podcasts
- Creating basic reports for the company, such as weekly tasks, sales, etc.
- Preparing slideshows for the company's upcoming presentations
- Liaising between yourself and other team members to ensure that everyone is on track with the work they

should be doing – keeping everyone on schedule for certain deadlines

- Recruiting new team members for the company and, in some cases, training them to do their jobs
- Setting up social media accounts and keeping them optimized
- Managing and updating social media accounts on a regular basis
- Managing and setting up blogs
- Publishing blog posts that you have provided
- Filtering and replying to comments on your blog
- Answering support tickets with a platform like Zendesk
- Commenting on your blog and other blogs to increase traffic to your blog
- Participating in discussion forums or message boards on behalf of your business to drive more traffic to your business or your website

Each of these tasks is something that can support a company with growing, yet is often more than a company has time for. Especially as a brand continues to grow, having enough time to contribute to things like this can be overwhelming. Offering your services is a great opportunity to help the company keep their smaller behind-the-scenes tasks running so that they can focus on bigger things like starting and running new projects, or offering services or products that are fundamental to the business itself.

How To Get Started

Getting started as a virtual assistant is easy: create a list of everything that you offer and begin reaching out to your network to see if you can meet with anyone who is willing to hire you, or recommend you to someone who is hiring a virtual assistant. You may need to have a few samples of your services available so that people know they can hire you and get work done through you, as samples tend to show people that you offer high quality work. Designing your website or certain features on your website yourself, or offering samples of your written work is a great opportunity for you to show people how good you are at your job. You can also consider asking your early clients to provide you with reviews or testimonials after you have worked together for a while, as having these testimonies often shows people that you are good at what you do and that you are guaranteed by other clients.

If you do not yet have a network of people who you can reach out to, consider using a platform like Upwork or Fiverr to get your first few jobs from so that you can accumulate experience and reviews. After that, however, make sure that you start getting clients on your own so that you are not paying a percentage of your work fees to every single person who you work with. You can also go ahead and start joining groups on Facebook where business folks hangout and otherwise growing your network online so that you begin to have people who know you as being a virtual assistant. The more you go ahead and create these connections, the more chances you have of being hired, so continue working toward building your network. Before you know it, you will have a full roster and you will no longer have to continue working toward building your network because you will have plenty of clients to work with!

How Successful You Will Be

The biggest key to generating success as a virtual assistant is getting your name out there and letting people get to know you for the work that you do. Many people have a lot of fear around marketing themselves early on which can lead to a slow start, so be brave in coming forth as a virtual assistant and continue sharing your work with people. Talk about your business and services as often as you reasonably can and continue to let people know about the work you do so that they can continue coming to you. The more that you share with people and grow your network, the more successful you will be.

Virtual assistants can charge anywhere from $1 to $100 per hour, with the average being between $20 - $50 per hour, depending on their skill and what they are offering to a company. This means that if you work about 15 hours per week as a virtual assistant, you can make anywhere from $1,200 to $3,000 per month as a virtual assistant. The more you work, obviously, the more you are going to earn, which will help you become even more successful.

How to Scale Your Business

Many virtual assistants will scale their businesses by offering more hours per week and taking on more clients. For virtual assistants who have a full client roster and who are charging on the higher end of the scale, often their virtual assistant work earns them more than their other work does so they may choose to go full time with it. This is one great opportunity to scale your business and earn more as a virtual assistant. If you want to continue keeping this as your side hustle, however, you can either increase your wages or begin creating virtual assistant packages. Many virtual assistants will create packages that feature certain specific services either one time only or as an ongoing monthly fee. If you do this, you can offer specialized services and charge a set fee then, if you get it done sooner, you end up being able to book more clients and earn more per month. For some virtual assistants, packages are an easier way to earn more per client as opposed to hourly wages.

How Long It Will Take To See Profits

Because virtual assistant work is something that does not take much financial investment to get started, most virtual assistants begin seeing profits in their first month as soon as they hire their first client. If you have a healthy enough network, you could start seeing profits in your business as high as $1,000+ per month as early as your first month. Many virtual assistants will offer exclusive savings offers to their first two or three clients so that they can get started working and accumulating experiences and reviews, which creates an added incentive for people to hire them. If you do this and you get all spots booked, you could earn as much as $1,200+ in your first month in business, depending on what your incentives are and how long people want to work with you on an hourly basis.

CHAPTER 20

SELL YOUR PHOTOGRAPHY SKILLS

Selling photography is something that many people dream of doing, yet not everyone really knows how to get started or how to earn a profit doing this type of work. There are actually two ways that you can earn a profit from your photography skills: through selling stock photographs, or through selling photography sessions. Both ways can earn you income on top of what you already make, and are based around your own hours and what you are willing to put into the work that you are planning on doing. If you are a photographer or you are at least decent with a camera, this may be a great opportunity for you to start earning money as a photographer.

Why Selling Your Photography Skills Works

People love looking at photographs, and photography is a popular niche skill that tends to earn a fair bit of money. If you love taking photographs but do not necessarily want to book sessions and photograph strangers, you can always go ahead and start taking photographs and selling them to stock photography websites like iStock or Getty Images. These are great platforms to use if you want to earn a profit, and they work because graphic marketing is a powerful tool yet many people are terrible at taking high quality images for their businesses. Rather than doing it themselves, many people will simply purchase stock photographs from the internet and use these, which makes it easier for them to get plenty of high quality images for their website and social media accounts. If you love taking high quality images of random things or landscapes, this can be a great way to sell those images for a profit, rather than letting them eat up space on a hard drive.

If you do love taking photographs of people, or even of their animals or of their products for businesses, selling your photography skills as sessions is another great opportunity for you to earn a profit as a photographer. Many people will book clients in for customized sessions which is a great opportunity to earn a large amount of cash per session. This does tend to yield higher earnings for the photographer; however, it also does require you to be willing to have in-person sessions with people and their families, pets, or businesses.

What You Need To Get Started With Selling Stock Photographs

If you want to get started selling stock photographs, all you need is a high quality camera, a photo editing software like Photoshop, and an account with a stock photograph website or a few if you want to sell on multiple platforms. If you do not have any of the required equipment at all, getting started selling stock photography can cost you anywhere from $1,500 to $10,000, depending on what camera you buy and what quality of lenses and flashes you choose. Typically, this is a better option for people who already have a camera and who are hobby photographers who would like to earn some extra cash from their hobby.

How To Get Started Selling Stock Photographs

Once you have your necessary equipment, all you need to do to start selling stock photographs is take high quality images, edit them, and upload them to sell them on stock image websites. You will likely have to input certain keywords and metatags (a fancy name for a certain type of keyword) with your photograph so that the stock image website knows when to show your photographs to potential buyers. Then, anytime an individual or a business purchases your stock photograph you earn a percentage of the sale. Other than this, all you need to do is regularly upload new images and keep your payment information up to date so that the platform can transfer you your earnings.

What You Need to Get Started Selling Photography Sessions

If you want to earn more money as a photographer, selling photography sessions is the best way to go. With photography sessions, you can take photographs of people, boudoir, weddings, families, newborns, businesses, or even animals for people. You can offer whatever type of photography sessions you want and can act either as a jack of all trades type photographer, or one who specializes in a certain type of photography. How you choose to arrange this and what type of photography you choose to take is entirely up to you.

In order to get started as a photographer, you will need a high quality camera with proper lenses and flashes, a high quality photo editing software, a website that shows off your work and your skills, and a marketing strategy to reach potential clients. To get all of this set up you will likely need to invest $5,000+ into your business, so understand that it is a fairly expensive business to get started in. Many photographers will also offer props such as backdrops and certain costume pieces for photography sessions so that their clients can have fun themes or pretty backdrops for their sessions. If you want to do this, that will be an added expense ranging from $200 upward.

How to Get Started Selling Photography Sessions

After you have invested in everything you need to get started, selling your photography sessions only requires a strong marketing plan. Typically, the best way to get started is to take some sample photographs for people that you already know and then create an online portfolio for people to look at. This is a great way for people to get some free or inexpensive photographs while you also get some samples to show your clients how good you are at what you do. Once you have a portfolio built, you can begin sharing your skills with people and encouraging them to purchase your sessions. Some photographers will offer discounted sessions at first to increase bookings and then will offer official rates after. Once you have had your initial clients booked, you can use their reviews and, with permission, photographs from their sessions in your portfolio for future bookings. This way, you can continue getting more bookings. Generally, the best way to get out there as a photographer is through word of mouth, so make sure that you keep talking and encouraging people who have worked with you to keep talking, too!

How Successful You Will Be

How successful you will be as a photographer depends on what type of photography you choose to do with your skills. If you choose to sell stock photography, you are likely going to make around $500 per month, assuming that you have a healthy number of images uploaded into a stock platform. To earn $500 per month, you will need about 80-100 high quality images uploaded. You can earn more by having high quality images that are relevant and that are useful to people. The more trending your photographs are, the more likely they are going to be picked against the competition, so focus on uploading stuff that people actually want.

As a photographer selling photography sessions, working part time you can earn as much as $1,200 per month, as each session generally sells for upward of $125. Some people even earn more by offering professional hair and makeup services and selling packages, in which case you can earn upward of $300+ per package. This is a great opportunity for you to profit from your photography skills and earn a significant income despite only investing a few hours per month into your business. To give you an idea, the average boudoir photographer will earn $600 per package, with the package being about 3 hours long and including hair and makeup services. If you had four per month, you could be earning $2,400 per month with just 24 hours of work (this includes editing time.) If you were a wedding photographer, you could charge an average of $1,000 per session, which could be $4,000 per month if you had one wedding per week.

How to Scale Your Business

Scaling your photography business is simple: take more photographs. If you want to earn more on your stock images, take more images and upload them. Many photographers who offer professional sessions will often take images for fun or for practice and will edit them and then upload them as stock images as a way to earn an extra income. If you do this and you practice and upload regularly, you could be earning $500+ per month just from your practice photography, on top of everything else that you are doing. Over time, as your image count grows, you could be earning $1,000+ this way.

If you want to scale your business taking professional photographs, the best way is to offer great packages and increase your positive ratings. The more that you are recommended by others, the more you are going to earn as a photographer. You can also develop an online presence using social media platforms like Instagram that thrive on image sharing, as this is a great opportunity to promote your skills. Another way that people will increase their photography bookings is by offering mini sessions, where they choose a location and then go there for 8 hours and book clients for inexpensive 30 minute sessions ranging from $50 - $300 per session. If you were to book out all 16 30 minute sessions, even just at $50 a piece you would earn $800 that day. This is a great opportunity to book out otherwise slow days and continue earning more from your business.

Another way that people can scale their photography business and potentially earn money is through entering contests. Although this is not a guaranteed way to win money, many photographers enter contests and, when they win, earn some sort of cash for their winnings. Alternatively, you could print your favorite images and offer them to your clients as prints to hang in their house. There are many ways that photography can be offered as a service, so get creative and look for more opportunities to get your photography into other peoples' hands! The more you offer, the more you stand to make.

How Long It Will Take To See Profits

Because photography is such an expensive business to get into, it typically takes people 6-12 months to earn a profit from their business, longer if they are selling stock photographs as opposed to actual sessions. If you want to see your profit back as soon as possible, doing both stock images and professional sessions is the best opportunity to make your money back as soon as possible. The more you offer and the more time you have available, the better. Be sure to really leverage word of mouth and focus on building a high quality portfolio so that people are more inspired to hire you, as this is the best way to grow your business rapidly which means you get more bookings early on.

CONCLUSION

Congratulations on completing *Side Hustle!*

If you are ready to start increasing your income, getting a side hustle is a great opportunity for you to earn extra cash on top of what you are already earning every month. Earning money is a great opportunity for you to have more funds to play with, to pay off debt with, or even to invest if you are ready to start growing bigger funds for yourself or your family! Having more money is always a great thing, so choosing to invest your time in finding a way to produce a greater income for yourself is a genius opportunity to get yourself ahead in life.

I hope that by reading *Side Hustle* you were able to get a strong idea about what is available to you and how you can get started. Believe it or not, side hustles really do not have to be that challenging to get started. As well, anyone can do them! There is nothing stopping you from going ahead and getting your own side hustle started, any more than there is another person. The people who are already doing it are people who are just like you, only they have already taken the leap. You can do it too!

After reading this book, I encourage you to pick just one side hustle that you are interested in and that you can afford with your present budget and get started on it. You can invest your time into growing and perfecting that hustle until you have generated enough income and made it stable enough that you can go ahead and start another one. Continuing to stack your side hustles on top of one another, especially the passive or semi-passive ones, is a great opportunity for you to make the maximum amount possible with as little time possible, too. The more you continue developing and maturing these opportunities, the more you are going to earn without having to put in so much work! This is a great way to eventually retire your 9-to-5 lifestyle if that is what you desire and get on board with making a livable income *right now*, while also having the time freedom to actually enjoy yourself!

Lastly, if you felt that you enjoyed this book and got plenty of value from it, please consider leaving an honest review of it. Your feedback would be greatly appreciated.

Thank you, and good luck with your hustle!

www.ingramcontent.com/pod-product-compliance
Lightning Source LLC
Chambersburg PA
CBHW071434210326
41597CB00020B/3795